The Don't Laugh Challenge ™

8 YEAR OLD EDITION

Don't Laugh Challenge
BONUS PLAY

Join our Joke Club and get the Bonus Play PDF!

Simply send us an email to:

 bacchuspublish@gmail.com

and you will get the following:

• **10 BONUS** hilarious jokes!

• An entry in our **Monthly Giveaway** of a
$25 Amazon Gift card!

We draw a new winner each month and will contact you via email!

Good luck!

Welcome to
The Don't Laugh Challenge ™

• How do you play?

The Don't Laugh Challenge is made up of 10 rounds with
2 games in each round. It is a 2-3 player game with the
players being 'Jester #1','Jester #2', and a 'King' or
'Queen'. In each game you have an opportunity to score
points by making the other players laugh.

After completing each round, tally up the points to
determine the Round Champion! Add all 10 rounds
together to see who is the Ultimate Don't Laugh
Challenge Master! If you end up in a tie, use our final Tie
Breaker Round for a Winner Takes All!

• Who can play the game?

Get the whole family involved! Grab a family member or
a friend and take turns going back and forth. We've also
added Bonus Points in game 2, so grab a 3rd person,
a.k.a 'King' or 'Queen', and earn an extra point by making
them guess your scene!

BILLY BOY

The Don't Laugh Challenge™
Activity Rules

- ## Game 1 - Jokes (1 point each)

  Jester #1 will hold the book and read each joke to
  Jester #2. If the joke makes Jester #2 laugh, Jester #1
  can record a point for the joke. Each joke is worth 1
  point. At the end of the jokes, tally up your total Joke
  Points scored for Jester #1 and continue to Game 2!

- ## Game 2 - Silly Scenarios
  ## (2 points each + bonus point)

  Without telling the other Jester what the scenarios say,
  read each scenario to yourself and then get creative by
  acting it out! You can use sound effects, but be sure not
  to say any words! If you make the other Jester laugh,
  record your points and continue to the next scenario.

  BONUS POINT: Get your parents or a third player, a.k.a
  King or Queen, involved and have them guess what in the
  world you are doing! Get the King or Queen to guess
  the scene correctly and you score a BONUS POINT!

The Don't Laugh Challenge ™
Activity Rules

Once Jester #1 completes both games it is Jester #2's turn. The directions at the bottom of the book will tell you who goes next. Once you have both completed all the games in the round, add your total points from each game to the Round Score Page and record the Round winner!

• How do you get started?

Flip a coin. If guessed correctly, then that Jester begins!

Tip: Make any of the activities extra funny by using facial expressions, funny voices or silly movements!

ROUND
1

Jokes

What did the monkey do when he found out he won the lottery?

He went BANANAS!

_____ /1

What do spiders study in college?

WEB Design.

_____ /1

How did the karate pig break a board?

With a Pork-CHOP!

_____ /1

What type of candy is an old lady's favorite?

Kit-CATS!

_____ /1

JOKES TOTAL: _____ /4

JESTER 1 CONTINUE TO THE NEXT PAGE ➡

Silly Scenarios

(Act it out!)

You are a friendly snake sliding along the floor when you slide into some itching powder! The problem is you don't have hands! Do your best to scratch those itches on anything you can find!

/2

Pretend you're a crazy cat lady who likes to sit in your rocking chair and talk to the cats. Show where they are by petting or talking to them - they can be on your head, shoulders, or lap!

/2

SILLY SCENARIOS TOTAL: _____ /4

NOW, PASS THE BOOK TO JESTER 2 ➜

Jokes

What did the dancing dentist recommend?

Flossin' every day! ___ /1

What's the handyman's favorite fruit?

A re-PEAR. ___ /1

What kind of bugs like to read?

BOOKworms! ___ /1

What is a shark's favorite candy?

JAW-colate. ___ /1

JOKES TOTAL: ___ /4

JESTER 2 CONTINUE TO THE NEXT PAGE →

14

Silly Scenarios

(Act it out!)

Oh no, your favorite toy has been kidnapped! To rescue it, cross a hall of invisible laser beams, by any means necessary - crouching, crawling, or even rolling!

/2

Imagine you're a scuba diver exploring the depths of the ocean, but instead of water, it's a sticky ocean made of honey!

/2

SILLY SCENARIOS TOTAL: _____ /4

TIME TO SCORE YOUR POINTS! ➡️

JESTER 1

/8

ROUND TOTAL

JESTER 2

/8

ROUND TOTAL

ROUND CHAMPION

ROUND 2

Jokes

What happened when a porcupine fell in love with a cactus?

It was a STICK-y situation.

/1

What did Batman say after he got sprayed by a skunk?

"To the Bat Tub!"

/1

What do you call a tree that has hands?

A palm tree.

/1

Why did the astronaut quit his job?

He heard the sky is the limit!

/1

JOKES TOTAL: _____ /4

Silly Scenarios

(Act it out!)

You shoot an arrow into the air, but it aims for you when it comes back down... RUN!!!!

_____ /2

You forgot to bring bug spray on the camping trip, and mosquitos are everywhere! You swat and slap them frantically - anything to keep from getting bitten!

_____ /2

SILLY SCENARIOS TOTAL: _____ /4

 NOW, PASS THE BOOK TO JESTER 2 ➡

19

Jokes

What animal has an arm, but no hands?

Armadillo!

/1

What does whipped cream say, when you put it on a slice of pie?

"Foam, sweet foam!"

/1

What type of shirt does a farmer wear?

A crop top!

/1

What TV shows are the cleanest?

Soap Operas.

/1

JOKES TOTAL: _____ /4

Silly Scenarios

(Act it out!)

You are playing football and just made the winning touchdown. Now you have to show off your best **VICTORY DANCE!**

_____ /2

You've just prepared a baked potato fresh from the oven. As you try to get the extremely hot potato onto your plate, it barely touches you and **OUCH!** It's **HOT!** Pretend to drop it and get it back on your plate, without burning yourself again!

_____ /2

SILLY SCENARIOS TOTAL: _____ /4

TIME TO SCORE YOUR POINTS! ➜

21

JESTER 1

/8
ROUND TOTAL

JESTER 2

/8
ROUND TOTAL

ROUND
CHAMPION

ROUND
3

Jokes

What kind of magazines do cars read?
LIMO-zines.

/1

Why did the sun decide to become a movie actor?
It was born a star!

/1

What is a vampire's favorite type of plant?
A SUCK-ulent.

/1

How do you know when computers are hungry?
They take MEGA-bites!

/1

JOKES TOTAL: _____ /4

Silly Scenarios

(Act it out!)

Show off your awesome break dancing skills... in **SLOW MOTION!!**

/2

You are a tight rope walker in the circus. You need to keep your balance on the rope, as you walk in a straight line with your arms out and your eyes closed. Try and take at least 10 steps without falling **OR** opening your eyes!

/2

SILLY SCENARIOS TOTAL: _____ /4

NOW, PASS THE BOOK TO JESTER 2 →

Jokes

What do you call a fusion of Texan and Mexican food made with Dinosaur meat?

/1

T-Rex Tex-Mex!

How does a banana answer the phone?

/1

"Yellow?"

What did the hand say to the sad fingers?

/1

"Snap out of it!"

Why didn't the tree talk to the bush?

/1

It didn't want to branch out.

JOKES TOTAL: _____ /4

JESTER 2 CONTINUE TO THE NEXT PAGE ➝

Silly Scenarios

(Act it out!)

You're reading the funniest book ever written, but you're in the library. Laugh hysterically, roll on the ground, hold your belly, and slap your knees - without making a sound!

 /2

A snake charmer is playing a mystical tune. Rise from your slumber by doing your slithery snake dance!

/2

SILLY SCENARIOS TOTAL: _____ /4

TIME TO SCORE YOUR POINTS! ➡

 **JESTER 1**  **/8**

ROUND TOTAL

 **JESTER 2**  **/8**

ROUND TOTAL

ROUND CHAMPION

ROUND
4

Jokes

How did the fart become King?

It was AIR to the throne!

/1

What famous band is known to be very flexible?

The Rubber Band!

/1

What dinosaur loves to eat meat the most?

A STEAK-osauraus!

/1

What should you do if a bird is flying at your head?

DUCK!

/1

JOKES TOTAL: _____ /4

Silly Scenarios

(Act it out!)

You are a clumsy cheerleader cheering for your favorite team! You tend to do things like trip over yourself and forget your dance moves, but you have to keep smiling no matter what!

_____ /2

Act like a baby chick hopping around catching snowflakes! Don't forget to peep once you get one!

_____ /2

SILLY SCENARIOS TOTAL: _____ /4

 NOW, PASS THE BOOK TO JESTER 2 ➡

Jokes

What can you make from trees on a beach?

SANDpaper.   /1

I asked my calculator for some help on my math homework. He said, "You can count on me!"

                                                  /1

What do pharmacists sleep on?

PILL-ows.   /1

What's the thieves favorite football team?

The Steelers.   /1

JOKES TOTAL: _____ /4

Silly Scenarios

(Act it out!)

You are being chased by a swarm of wasps!
Flail your arms and run for cover!

_____ /2

You are a cat getting ready to pounce! Focus on
something in the room like it's your target, get
low, and then... POUNCE!

_____ /2

SILLY SCENARIOS TOTAL: _____ /4

TIME TO SCORE YOUR POINTS! ➡

 **JESTER 1** /8
___
ROUND TOTAL

 **JESTER 2** /8
___
ROUND TOTAL

___
ROUND
CHAMPION

ROUND
5

Jokes

Why did the farmer put his cow on a rollercoaster?

He wanted to make a milkshake!

/1

Why did the broom fall asleep on the floor?

It was feeling very sweepy!

/1

How is Tarzan getting around these days?

Just vine.

/1

What do berries in a jar say to each other?

"Looks like we're in a jam!"

/1

JOKES TOTAL: _____ /4

Silly Scenarios

(Act it out!)

You are a playful little puppy and you love to chase your tail! Keep running in circles until you get so dizzy that you fall over!

_____ /2

You're walking your dog on his leash... when he suddenly he takes off running! Show how hard he's pulling you around the room and try to get him under control!

_____ /2

SILLY SCENARIOS TOTAL: _____ /4

NOW, PASS THE BOOK TO JESTER 2 ➡

Jokes

Why did the chef say she was throwing lettuce and tomatoes in the air?

She was making a tossed salad!

/1

What do you give a computer on its birthday?

GIF baskets!

/1

How do you know that magic makes you have to pee?

Well, why else are they called WIZ-ards!

/1

What did the astronaut say when he hit his head?

"I'm seeing stars!"

/1

JOKES TOTAL: _____ /4

Silly Scenarios

(Act it out!)

You're a baseball player who is trying to catch a ball, but when you finally catch it, it feels like it's 100 degrees! OUCH! Do your best not to drop it and get it to the next player or you'll lose the game point!

/2

Pretend you're a squirrel who accidentally ate all of your nuts before winter! Now with a giant belly, try and go hunt for more!

/2

SILLY SCENARIOS TOTAL: _____ /4

TIME TO SCORE YOUR POINTS! ➜

JESTER 1

/8

ROUND TOTAL

JESTER 2

/8

ROUND TOTAL

ROUND
CHAMPION

ROUND
6

Jokes

Why did the chef include a soccer shoe in his stew?

To give it a KICK!

/1

What do tires that are best friends say?

"Wheel always be together!"

/1

What do you call a drawing that makes you laugh?

A Snicker-doodle!

/1

Why was the jewelry salesman a good security guard?

He always kept WATCH.

/1

JOKES TOTAL: _____ /4

Silly Scenarios

(Act it out!)

You are a crab enjoying a nice walk on the beach, but people keep stepping around you! Make grumpy faces as you do your best impression of a walking crab dodging big feet.

_____ /2

You are a great big gorilla in the jungle. You are at a party with all of the other animals, and want to impress them with your dance moves!

_____ /2

SILLY SCENARIOS TOTAL: _____ /4

NOW, PASS THE BOOK TO JESTER 2 ➡

Jokes

Why are trees so obnoxious?
They never LEAF you alone!

/1

Why did the lamp get to skip a grade?
He was very bright!

/1

Why is the elevator so buff?
He lifts everyday!

/1

What do fish wear to weddings?
A Tux-SEA-do.

/1

JOKES TOTAL: _____ /4

Silly Scenarios

(Act it out!)

You're jumping rope by yourself, but the rope keeps getting tangled between your feet, so you start over. This time it gets so tangled you dramatially fall over and can't move!

 /2

You are a witch stirring yucky, stinky ingredients into your big cauldron for a spell. Give your best witchy laugh!

/2

SILLY SCENARIOS TOTAL: /4

TIME TO SCORE YOUR POINTS! ➜

 **JESTER 1**  **/8**

_____

ROUND TOTAL

 **JESTER 2**  **/8**

_____

ROUND TOTAL

_____

ROUND
CHAMPION

ROUND 7

Jokes

Why didn't the letters go swimming?

They couldn't find the C. (Sea)

/1

Why do flowers ride bikes?

They love to PETAL!

/1

What do you call a tropical bird that won't fly?

A Tou-can't.

/1

What happens when you put cheddar on an Apple computer?

You get Mac n' Cheese!

/1

JOKES TOTAL: _____ /4

Silly Scenarios

(Act it out!)

Pretend you're walking down the street on a rainy and windy day with an umbrella. Suddenly, a strong gust of wind pulls you backward! Try with all your might to hold onto your umbrella and move forward!

_____ /2

You are playing basketball with a very heavy ball. Try to dribble and shoot it even though it feels like it weighs a TON!

_____ /2

SILLY SCENARIOS TOTAL: _____ /4

NOW, PASS THE BOOK TO JESTER 2 ➡

Jokes

What fruit can help you drink a beverage?

A STRAW-berry!

/1

Why can't you trust a cloud?

They throw to much shade.

/1

Why did the guitar have to go to detention?

He was passing notes in class.

/1

What do you get when a poker playing prince uses the restroom?

A Royal Flush.

/1

JOKES TOTAL: _____ /4

JESTER 2 CONTINUE TO THE NEXT PAGE ➡

Silly Scenarios

(Act it out!)

Play "Twinkle Twinkle Little Star" as a heavy metal air guitarist.

_____ /2

While out ice skating with your family, you decide it's the right time to show them the new hula hoop tricks you've learned. When you try to show them, pretend to go out of control and fall with a surprised look on your face!

_____ /2

SILLY SCENARIOS TOTAL: _____ /4

TIME TO SCORE YOUR POINTS! ➜

JESTER 1

/8
ROUND TOTAL

JESTER 2

/8
ROUND TOTAL

ROUND CHAMPION

ROUND

8

Jokes

What's a surfer's favorite type of pizza?

Hawaiian!

/1

What animal likes to make fun of people?

A Mockingbird.

/1

What kind of money do crabs use?

Sand Dollars.

/1

How do you keep a crocodile from roaming around?

/1

Use an Alli-GATE-or!

JOKES TOTAL: _____ /4

Silly Scenarios

(Act it out!)

You take a big bite of something, but it turns out to be extra, **EXTRA** spicy! You fan your mouth and guzzle lots of water trying to cool down your tongue.

_____ /2

You're a lion who loves to play golf. Do a big golf swing and let out a roar... or four!

_____ /2

SILLY SCENARIOS TOTAL: _____ /4

NOW, PASS THE BOOK TO JESTER 2 ➡

Jokes

Where does the gardener kiss his wife?

On her TULIPS!   /1

What do you call a song about house cats?

A Meow-sical number.   /1

What is a cowboy's favorite salad dressing?

Ranch.   /1

What do you call it when your parents go to buy anchovies?

GROSS-ery shopping!   /1

JOKES TOTAL: _____ /4

Silly Scenarios

(Act it out!)

It's 'League Night' at the local bowling alley. Do your best-bowling arm swing to hit a strike and win the game!

_____ /2

You're a professional bull rider getting ready to ride. Remember to keep your balance and do your best to hold onto your hat, as this wild bull leaves its cage!

_____ /2

SILLY SCENARIOS TOTAL: _____ /4

TIME TO SCORE YOUR POINTS! ➔

JESTER 1

/8

ROUND TOTAL

JESTER 2

/8

ROUND TOTAL

ROUND CHAMPION

ROUND
9

Jokes

Why didn't the bear trust the trout?

He thought it seemed a little fishy.

/1

What is the wealthiest animal in the zoo?

The Ost-RICH!

/1

What do you call a lemon that's been saved from a tree?

Lemon-aid!

/1

What's a Jedi's favorite weapon in the office?

A screen-saber!

/1

JOKES TOTAL: ____ /4

Silly Scenarios

(Act it out!)

A bee lands on you in the middle of math class. Pretend to silently freak out while you desperately try to get it to leave, without disrupting the teacher or students!

/2

You are a chicken who starts to cross a busy road, but decides to direct traffic instead!

/2

SILLY SCENARIOS TOTAL: _____ /4

NOW, PASS THE BOOK TO JESTER 2 ➞

Jokes

What dessert can you make during an earthquake?

Milk-SHAKES!   /1

Why won't your hand ever grow to be 12 inches long?

Because then it would be a foot!   /1

Tina: "Mommy, my tooth is loose."

Mommy: "Well, you better go after it!"   /1

Do you have games on your phone?   /1

APP-solutely!

JOKES TOTAL: /4

Silly Scenarios

(Act it out!)

Act like a spider walking around, then slowly shriveling up on it's back.

_____ /2

You're a trumpet player doing a solo. Show how you can really get into your music!

_____ /2

SILLY SCENARIOS TOTAL: _____ /4

TIME TO SCORE YOUR POINTS! ➡️

 **JESTER 1**

/8

ROUND TOTAL

 **JESTER 2**

/8

ROUND TOTAL

ROUND
CHAMPION

ROUND
10

Jokes

Why wasn't Peter Pan good at flying an airplane?

Because he would Never-land!

/1

What kind of food does a bully snack on?

JERK-y.

/1

Why was the dog a good motivational speaker?

He was always so PAW-sitive!

/1

I thought picking my birthday dessert was going to be hard, but it was a piece of cake!

/1

JOKES TOTAL: _____ /4

JESTER 1 CONTINUE TO THE NEXT PAGE ➡

Silly Scenarios

(Act it out!)

You are brushing your very long hair, but it gets so tangled that you can't get your brush out. Do whatever it takes to get free of the brush!

_____ /2

You are a soldier in the middle of combat. You need to crawl through the trenches, throw your grenade, and shoot at the enemy without getting caught! Ready... GO!

_____ /2

SILLY SCENARIOS TOTAL: _____ /4

NOW, PASS THE BOOK TO JESTER 2 ➡

Jokes

What is the fruit's favorite city?

Minne-APPLE-is.   /1

What does the lettuce say to his friends to calm them down?

"ROMAINE calm!"   /1

Who is the sheep's favorite musician?

GOATS-art!   /1

Why did the chicken stay indoors?

The weather was foul.   /1

JOKES TOTAL: /4

Silly Scenarios

(Act it out!)

You are a big-eyed bird flying around the room, singing and squawking as loudly as you can!

/2

Act like a cute little bunny hopping around, then do the stop, drop, and roll!

/2

SILLY SCENARIOS TOTAL: _____ /4

TIME TO SCORE YOUR POINTS! ➡

 **JESTER 1**

/8

ROUND TOTAL

 **JESTER 2**

 **/8**

ROUND TOTAL

ROUND CHAMPION

ADD UP ALL YOUR POINTS FROM EACH ROUND.
THE PLAYER WITH THE MOST POINTS IS CROWNED
THE ULTIMATE LAUGH MASTER!

IN THE EVENT OF A TIE, CONTINUE TO THE ROUND
11 FOR THE TIE-BREAKER ROUND!

JESTER 1 _____

GRAND TOTAL

JESTER 2 _____

GRAND TOTAL

_____

**THE ULTIMATE
DON'T LAUGH CHALLENGE MASTER**

ROUND

11

TIE-BREAKER
(WINNER TAKES ALL!)

Jokes

What do you get when you throw a big cat in the ocean?

A Sea Lion!

/1

Why do rhinos travel in packs?

Because it's not 'Rhinocer-ME'. It's 'Rhinocer-US'.

/1

What food is best at conversations?

Talk-o's! (Tacos)

/1

Why do kids love swimming in the river?

Unlimited streaming!

/1

JOKES TOTAL: _____ /4

Silly Scenarios

(Act it out!)

Pretend you're hammering a nail into the wall when you accidentally hammer your finger! OUCH!

_____ /2

You're getting ready to eat an invisible hot dog. Add some toppings, chow down, and act out how delicious it is!

_____ /2

SILLY SCENARIOS TOTAL: _____ /4

NOW, PASS THE BOOK TO JESTER 2 →

75

Jokes

What bird is always sad?

A Blue Jay.

/1

What do you call a mountain lion on a stick?

A Ka-bobcat!

/1

What kind of cake did the mouse have for its party?

CHEESE-cake.

/1

Why do kangaroos love Caprisun?

Because it comes in a pouch!

/1

JOKES TOTAL: _____ /4

JESTER 2 CONTINUE TO THE NEXT PAGE ➞

Silly Scenarios

(Act it out!)

You are a crab who loves to steal peoples food! Sneak up to grab it and then scuttle away with your sideways crab walk!

_____ /2

You are Secret Agent Zero. Sneak around during a mission with a bad case of gas... LOUD gas!

_____ /2

SILLY SCENARIOS TOTAL: _____ /4

TIME TO SCORE YOUR POINTS! ➜

ADD UP ALL YOUR POINTS FROM THE PREVIOUS ROUND. THE JESTER WITH THE MOST POINTS IS CROWNED THE ULTIMATE DON'T LAUGH CHALLENGE MASTER!

JESTER 1

/8

_____

GRAND TOTAL

JESTER 2

/8

_____

GRAND TOTAL

_____

THE ULTIMATE
DON'T LAUGH CHALLENGE MASTER

Check out our

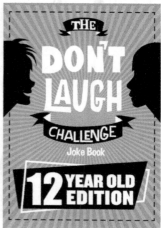

Visit us at
www.DontLaughChallenge.com
to check out our newest books!

other joke books!

If you have enjoyed our book, we would love for you to review us on Amazon!

Made in the USA
Middletown, DE
25 October 2021